Arthur Sullivan, Ernest Ford

**Vocal score of Utopia Limited, or, The flowers of progress**

an original comic opera in two acts

Arthur Sullivan, Ernest Ford

**Vocal score of Utopia Limited, or, The flowers of progress**
*an original comic opera in two acts*

ISBN/EAN: 9783743376878

Manufactured in Europe, USA, Canada, Australia, Japa

Cover: Foto ©Thomas Meinert / pixelio.de

Manufactured and distributed by brebook publishing software (www.brebook.com)

Arthur Sullivan, Ernest Ford

**Vocal score of Utopia Limited, or, The flowers of progress**

OF

# UTOPIA

## *LIMITED*

OR,

## THE FLOWERS OF PROGRESS.

### An Original Comic Opera,

IN TWO ACTS,

WRITTEN BY

# W. S. GILBERT

COMPOSED BY

# ARTHUR SULLIVAN

*Joint Authors of* "*Thespis; or, The Gods Grown Old*"; "*Trial by Jury*"; "*The Sorcerer*";
"*H.M.S. Pinafore; or, The Lass that Loved a Sailor*"; "*The Pirates of Penzance; or, The Slave of Duty*";
"*Patience; or, Bunthorne's Bride*"; "*Iolanthe; or, The Peer and the Peri*"; "*Princess Ida; or, Castle
Adamant*"; "*The Mikado; or, The Town of Titipu*"; "*Ruddigore; or, The Witch's Curse*";
"*The Yeomen of the Guard; or, The Merryman and his Maid*"; *and* "*The Gondoliers;
or, The King of Barataria.*"

ARRANGED FROM THE FULL SCORE BY

## ERNEST FORD.

| | | | |
|---|---|---|---|
| Vocal Score, complete | ... net 5s. 0d. | Pianoforte Solo | ... net 3s. 0d. |
| Ditto (bound) | ,, 7s. 6d. | Libretto | ,, 1s. 0d. |

### London:

## CHAPPELL & CO., 50, NEW BOND STREET, W.

AGENTS—NEW YORK: NOVELLO, EWER & CO.

*All Rights reserved under the International Copyright Act. Public Performance forbidden, and Right of Representation reserved. Single detached numbers may be sung at Concerts, not more than two at any one Concert, but they must be given without Costume or Action. In no case must such performances be announced as a "Selection" from the Opera. Applications for the right of performing the above Opera must be made to "*MR. D'OYLY CARTE, *Savoy Theatre, London.*"

COPYRIGHT, MDCCCXCIII, BY CHAPPELL & CO.

LONDON:
HENDERSON & SPALDING, LIMITED, PRINTERS,
3 AND 5, MARYLEBONE LANE, W.

First performed at the Savoy Theatre, London, under the management of Mr. D'Oyly Carte, on Saturday, October 7th, 1893.

# UTOPIA
## LIMITED
### THE FLOWERS OF PROGRESS.
*or,*

#### Dramatis Personæ.

| | |
|---|---|
| KING PARAMOUNT THE FIRST (*King of Utopia*) | ... MR. RUTLAND BARRINGTON. |
| SCAPHIO } (*Judges of the Utopian Supreme Court*) | MR. W. H. DENNY. |
| PHANTIS } | MR. JOHN LE HAY. |
| TARARA (*the Public Exploder*) | MR. WALTER PASSMORE. |
| CALYNX (*the Utopian Vice-Chamberlain*) | MR. BOWDEN HASWELL. |

IMPORTED FLOWERS OF PROGRESS.

| | |
|---|---|
| LORD DRAMALEIGH (*a British Lord Chamberlain*) | MR. SCOTT RUSSELL. |
| CAPTAIN FITZBATTLEAXE (*First Life Guards*) | MR. CHARLES KENNINGHAM |
| CAPTAIN SIR EDWARD CORCORAN, K.C.B. (*of the Royal Navy*) | MR. LAWRENCE GRIDLEY. |
| MR. GOLDBURY (*a Company Promoter*) | MR. SCOTT FISHE. |
| (*afterwards Comptroller of the Utopian Household.*) | |
| SIR BAILEY BARRE, Q.C., M.P. | MR. ENES BLACKMORE. |
| MR. BLUSHINGTON (*of the County Council*) | MR. HERBERT RALLAND. |

| | |
|---|---|
| THE PRINCESS ZARA (*Eldest Daughter of King Paramount*) | MISS NANCY McINTOSH. |
| THE PRINCESS NEKAYA } (*her Younger Sisters*) | MISS EMMIE OWEN. |
| THE PRINCESS KALYBA } | MISS FLORENCE PERRY. |
| THE LADY SOPHY (*their English Gouvernante*) | MISS ROSINA BRANDRAM. |
| SALATA } | MISS EDITH JOHNSTON. |
| MELENE } (*Utopian Maidens*) | MISS MAY BELL. |
| PHYLLA } | MISS FLORENCE EASTON. |

ACT I.—A UTOPIAN PALM GROVE
ACT II.—THRONE ROOM IN KING PARAMOUNT'S PALACE

MR. HAWES CRAVEN
(By permission of MR. HENRY IRVING).

Stage Director    MR. CHARLES HARRIS.
Musical Director    MR. FRANÇOIS CELLIER.

Stage Manager, MR. W. H. SEYMOUR. The Dances arranged by MR. JOHN D'AUBAN. The Utopian Dresses designed by MR. PERCY ANDERSON, and executed by MISS FISHER, MDME. AUGUSTE, and MDME. LÉON. Uniforms by Messrs. FIRMIN & SONS, also by MR. B. J. SIMMONS and Messrs. ANGEL & SONS. The Presentations by MDME. ISABEL BIZET-MICHAU. The Court Dresses by Messrs. RUSSELL & ALLEN. The Judges' Robes by Messrs. EDE & SON. The Ladies' Jewels by THE PARISIAN DIAMOND COMPANY. The Wigs by MR. CLARKSON. The Properties by MR. SKELLY. Stage Machinist, MR. P. WHITE.

The Opera produced under the sole direction of the Author and Composer.

# CONTENTS.

## Act I.

| NO. | | PAGE |
|---|---|---|
| 1. Chorus and Solo (*Phylla*) | "In lazy languor" | 1 |
| 2. Chorus | "O make way for the Wise Men" | 4 |
|     *a.* Duet (*Scaphio and Phantis*) with *Chorus* | "In every mental lore" | 6 |
| 3. Duet and Dance (*Scaphio and Phantis*) | "Let all your doubts take wing" | 11 |
| 4. Chorus with Solos | "Quaff the nectar" | 14 |
|     *a.* Song (*King*) with *Chorus* | "A King of autocratic power we" | 17 |
|     *b.* Duet (*Nekaya and Kalyba*) | "Although of native maids the cream" | 21 |
|     *c.* Valse Song (*Lady Sophy*) with *Chorus* | "Bold-faced ranger" | 25 |
| 5. Song (*King, with Scaphio and Phantis*) | "First you're born" | 30 |
| 6. Duet (*King and Lady Sophy*) | "Subjected to your heavenly gaze" | 34 |
| 7. Chorus with Solos (*Zara, Fitz., and Troopers*) | "Oh, maiden rich" | 38 |
| 8. Chorus with Solos (*Zara and Fitz.*) | "Ah! gallant soldier" | 45 |
| 9. Quartet (*Zara, Fitz., Scaphio, and Phantis*) | "It's understood, I think" | 50 |
| 10. Duet (*Zara and Fitz.*) | "Oh, admirable art" | 56 |
| 11. Finale | "Although your Royal summons to appear" | 60 |
|     *a.* Valse Song (*Zara*) with *Chorus* | "What these may be" | 67 |
|     *b.* Song (*Capt. Corcoran*) with *Chorus* | "I'm Captain Corcoran, K.C.B." | 74 |
|     *c.* Song (*Mr. Goldbury*) with *Chorus* | "Some seven men form an Association" | 83 |

## Act II.

| | | |
|---|---|---|
| 12. Recit. and Song (*Fitz.*) | "Oh, Zara!" and "A tenor, all singers above" | 95 |
| 13. Duet (*Zara and Fitz.*) | "Words of love too loudly spoken" | 98 |
| 14. Song (*King*) | "Society has quite forsaken" | 100 |
| 15. Entrance of Court | | 104 |
| 16. Drawing Room Music | | 105 |
| 17. Unaccompanied Chorus | "Eagle high on cloudland soaring" | 109 |
| 18. Duet (*Scaphio and Phantis*) | "With fury deep we burn" | 118 |
| 19. Trio (*King, Scaphio, and Phantis*) | "If you think that when banded" | 120 |
| 20. Trio (*Scaphio, Phantis, and Tarara*) | "With wily brain" | 124 |
| 21. Song (*Mr. Goldbury*) | "A wonderful joy our eyes to bless" | 131 |
| 22. Quartet (*Nek., Kal., Lord D., and Mr. Gold.*) | "Then I may sing and play?" | 135 |
| 23. Recit. and Song } (*Lady Sophy*) | "Oh, would some demon power" / "When but a maid" | 142 |
| 24. Recit. (*King and Lady Sophy*) | "Ah, Lady Sophy" | 144 |
|     *a.* Duet (*King and Lady Sophy*) | "Oh, the rapture unrestrained" | 146 |
|     *b.* Tarantella | | 149 |
| 25. Chorus | "Upon our sea-girt land" | 151 |
| 26. Finale | "There's a little group of isles" | 153 |

No. 2. **CHORUS.**

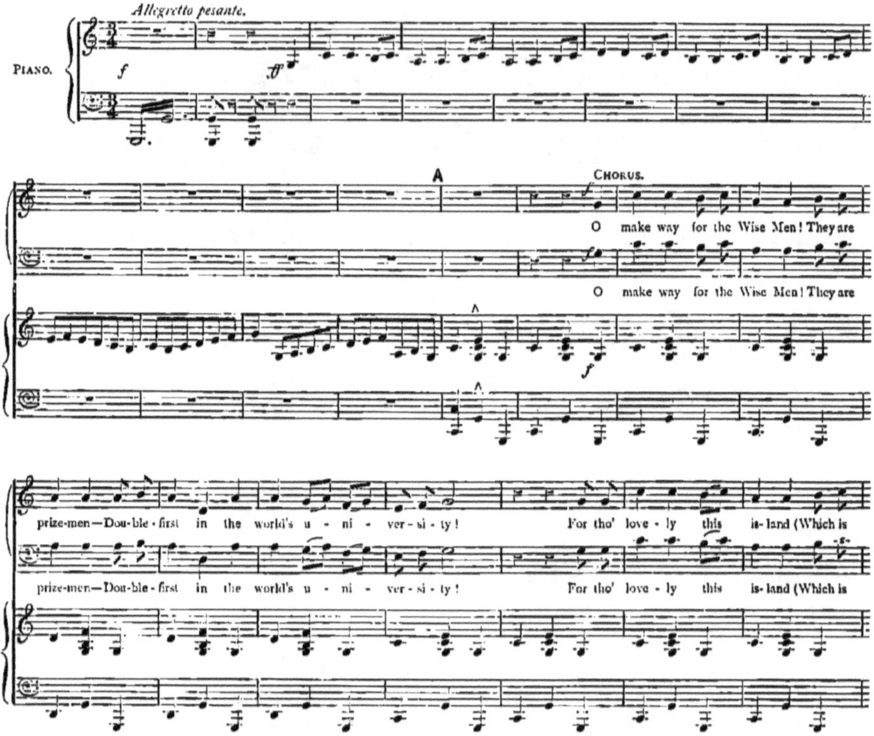
Allegretto pesante.
PIANO.
f
ff
A
CHORUS.
O make way for the Wise Men! They are
O make way for the Wise Men! They are
f
prize-men—Dou-ble-first in the world's u - ni - ver-si-ty! For tho' love-ly this is-land (Which is
prize-men—Dou-ble-first in the world's u - ni - ver-si-ty! For tho' love-ly this is-land (Which is
B
my land), She has no one to match them in her ci-ty. They're the pride of U - to-pia—Cor-nu -
my land), She has no one to match them in her ci-ty. They're the pride of U - to-pia—Cor-nu -

No. 3.     DUET—with Dance—(Scaphio & Phantis).

No. 4.   CHORUS with SOLOS.

No. 5.    SONG—(King, with Scaphio & Phantis).

No. 6. DUET—(Lady Sophy & King).

## No. 7. CHORUS—with SOLOS—(Zara, Captain Fitzbattleaxe, & Four Troopers).

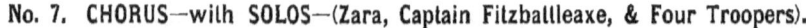

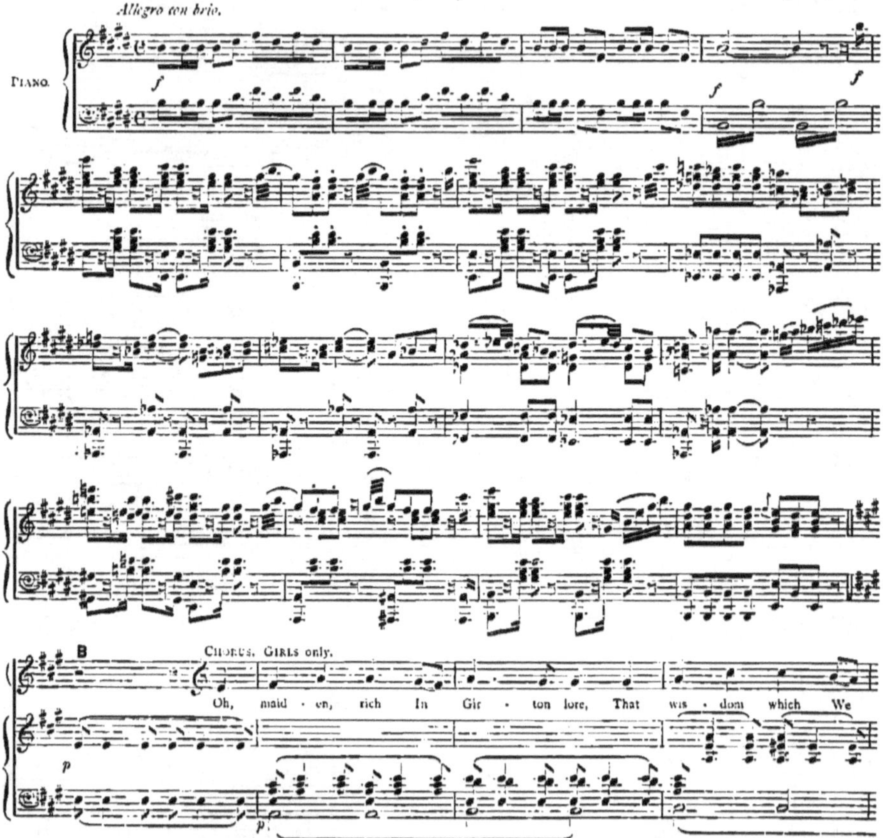
Allegro con brio.
Piano.
B
Chorus. Girls only.
Oh, maid - en, rich In Gir - ton lore, That wis - dom which We
prized be - fore, We do con - fess Is no - thing-ness, And ra - ther less Per - haps, than

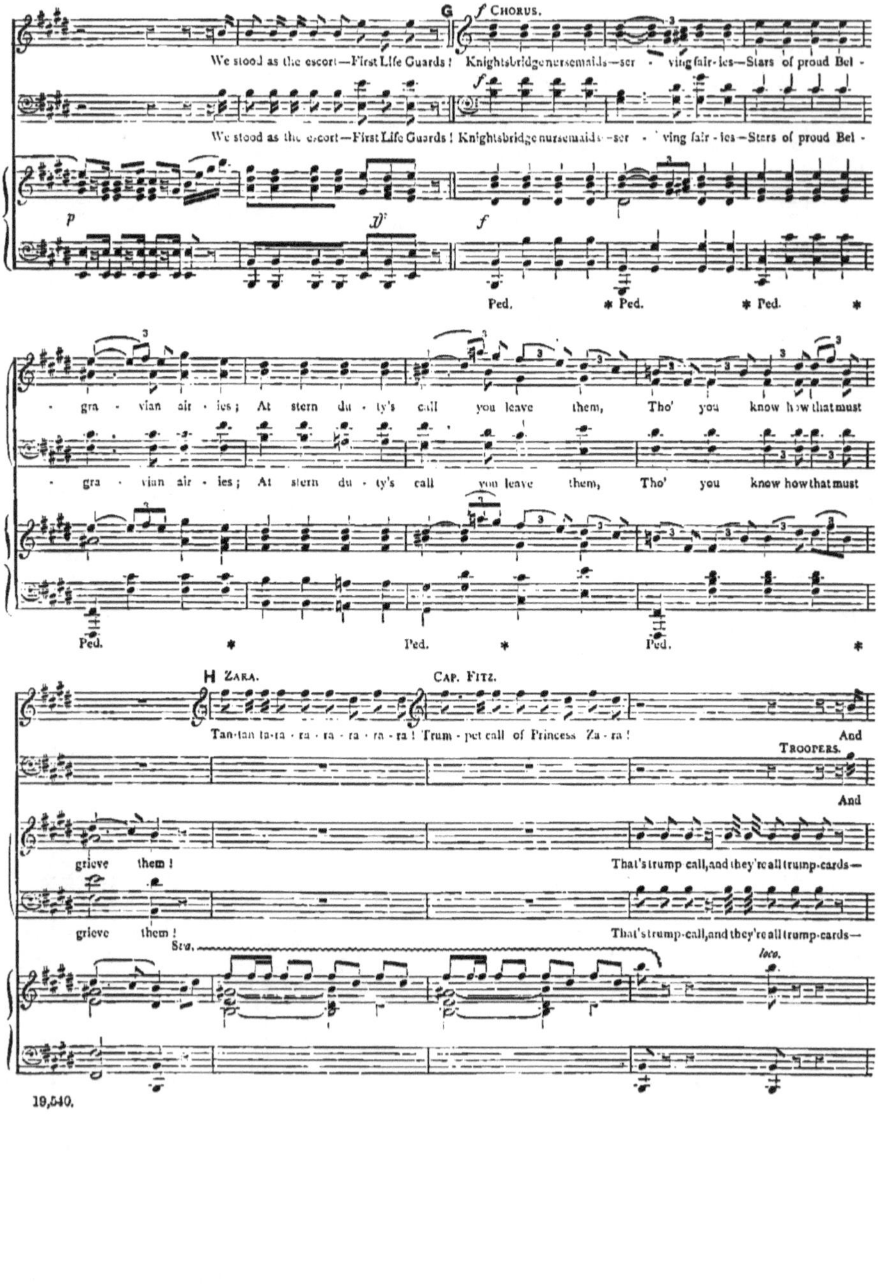
G
f CHORUS.
We stood as the escort—First Life Guards! Knightsbridge nursemaids—ser - ving fair-ies—Stars of proud Bel -
We stood as the escort—First Life Guards! Knightsbridge nursemaids—ser - ving fair-ies—Stars of proud Bel -
p
f
f
Ped. * Ped. * Ped. *
- gra - vian air - ies; At stern du - ty's call you leave them, Tho' you know how that must
- gra - vian air - ies; At stern du - ty's call you leave them, Tho' you know how that must
Ped. * Ped. * Ped. *
H ZARA.
CAP. FITZ.
Tan-tan ta-ra - ra - ra - ra - ra - ra! Trum - pet call of Princess Za - ra!
And
TROOPERS.
And
grieve them!
That's trump call, and they're all trump-cards—
grieve them!
That's trump-call, and they're all trump-cards—
8va.
loco.

No. 8.   CHORUS with SOLOS—(Zara & Captain Fitzbattleaxe).

## No. 9. QUARTET—(Zara, Captain Fitzbattleaxe, Scaphio, & Phantis).

No. 10.     DUET—(Zara & Captain Fitzbattleaxe).

No. 11.   FINALE ACT I.

(No. 11a.)

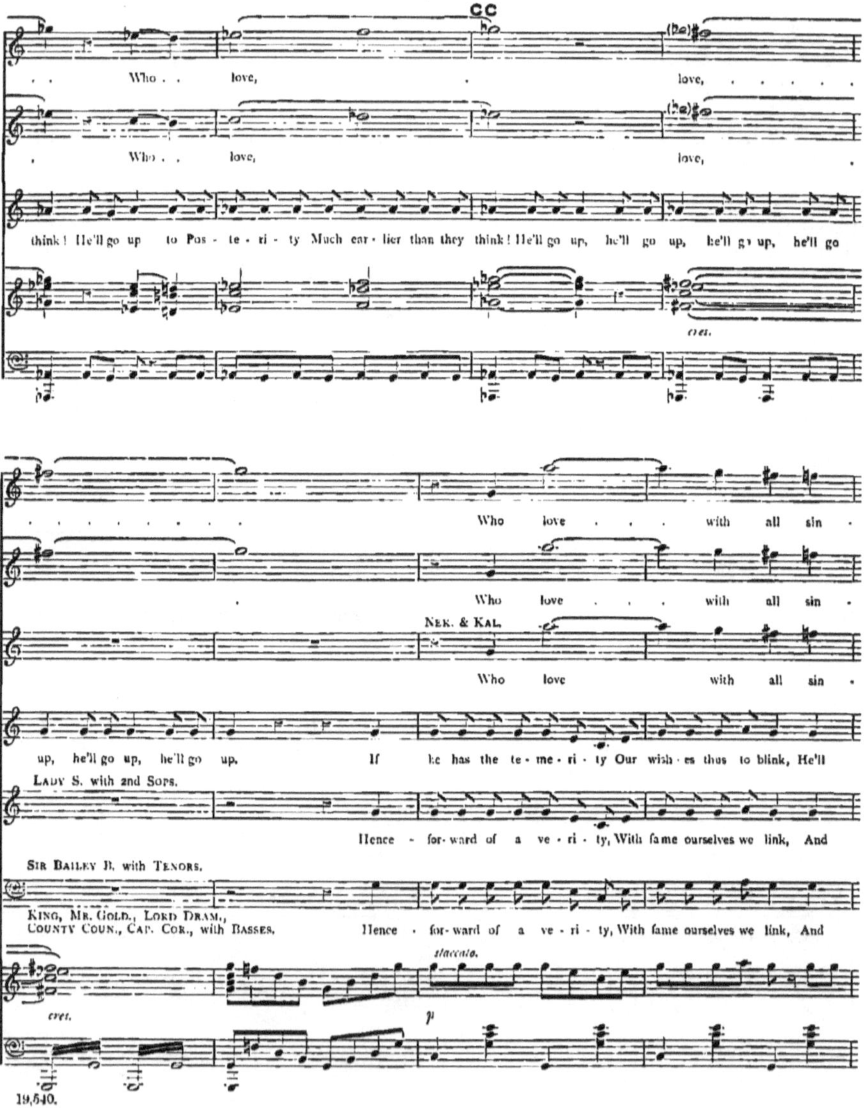
CC
. . Who . . love, . love, . . . . . .
. Who . . love, love, .
think! He'll go up to Pos - te - ri - ty Much ear - lier than they think! He'll go up, he'll go up, he'll go up, he'll go
cres.
. . . . . . . . Who love . . . with all sin -
. Who love . . . with all sin -
NEK. & KAL.
Who love with all sin -
up, he'll go up, he'll go up. If he has the te - me - ri - ty Our wish - es thus to blink, He'll
LADY S. with 2nd SOPS.
Hence - for - ward of a ve - ri - ty, With fame ourselves we link, And
SIR BAILEY B. with TENORS.
KING, MR. GOLD., LORD DRAM., COUNTY COUN., CAP. COR., with BASSES.
Hence - for - ward of a ve - ri - ty, With fame ourselves we link, And
staccato.
cres.
p

# ACT II.

**No. 12.** RECIT. & SONG—(Captain Fitzballleaxe).

No. 13. DUET—(Zara & Captain Fitzbattleaxe).

## No. 14. SONG—(King) with Chorus of Six Flowers of Progress—(Mr. Blush., Lord Dram., Sir B. Barre, Cap. Fitz., Mr. Gold., & Cap. Cor.).

## No. 15. ENTRANCE OF COURT.

No. 16.  DRAWING ROOM MUSIC.

No. 17.   RECIT.—(King) & CHORUS (Unaccompanied).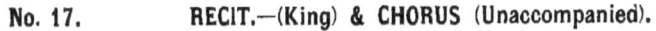

No. 19.     TRIO—(King, Scaphio, & Phantis).

### No. 20. TRIO—(Tarara, Phantis, & Scaphio).

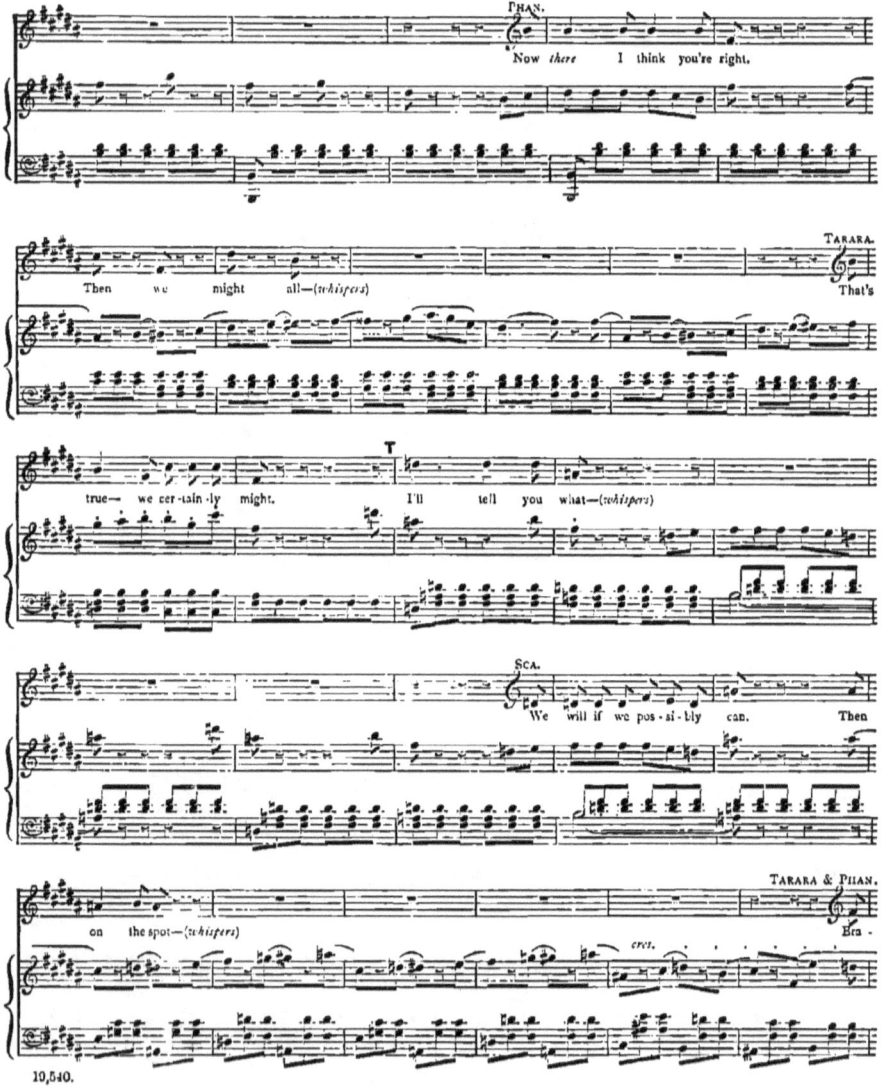

### No. 21.      SONG—(Mr. Goldbury).

## No. 22. QUARTET—(Nekaya, Kalyba, Lord Dramaleigh, & Mr. Goldbury).

No. 23. RECIT. & SONG—(Lady Sophy).

## No. 24. RECIT.—(King & Lady Sophy).

Ah, Lady Sophy— then you love me! For so you sing— No, no, by the stars that shine a-

bove me, Degraded King! For while these rumours, thro' the city

bruited, Remain uncontradicted, unrefuted, The object thou of my aversion

rooted, Repulsive thing! Be just— the time is now at hand When truth may

(No. 24a.) DUET—(King & Lady Sophy).

## TARANTELLA.

(No. 24b.)

No. 25. CHORUS.

No. 26.  FINALE ACT II.

# POPULAR SONGS
## By ARTHUR SULLIVAN.

|  | s. | d. |
|---|---|---|
| You sleep ("Serenade"), in C and D flat | 4 | 0 |
|   ,,   ,, (Italian words) E tu nol sai (Sung in "The Profligate") | 4 | 0 |
| If doughty deeds | 4 | 0 |
| A weary lot is thine, fair maid | 4 | 0 |
| The maiden's story | 4 | 0 |
| Arabian love song (in G minor and A minor) | 4 | 0 |
| I heard the nightingale (in F and A flat) | 4 | 0 |
| Thou'rt passing hence | 4 | 0 |
| Thou art weary (D minor and E minor) | 4 | 0 |
| The distant shore (in E flat, F, and G) | 4 | 0 |
| Sweethearts (in A flat and B flat) | 4 | 0 |
| Tender and true (in E flat and F) | 4 | 0 |
| Ever (in B flat, C, D flat, and E flat) | 4 | 0 |
| The Lady of the Lake | 4 | 0 |

*For other Songs see Operas, &c., by this Composer.*

London:
CHAPPELL & CO., 50, NEW BOND ST., W.

www.ingramcontent.com/pod-product-compliance
Lightning Source LLC
Chambersburg PA
CBHW030300170426
43202CB00009B/823